Asylum Road

MARY O'MALLEY

salmonpoetry

Also by Mary O'Malley

POETRY

A Consideration of Silk, Salmon Publishing, 1990.

Where the Rocks Float, Salmon Publishing, 1993.

The Knife in the Wave, Salmon Publishing, 1997.

Published in 2001 by
Salmon Publishing Ltd,
Cliffs of Moher, Co. Clare, Ireland
http://www.salmonpoetry.com
email: info@salmonpoetry.com

ISBN 1 903392 13 6   Paperback

The Arts Council   Salmon Publishing gratefully acknowledges the financial
An Chomhairle Ealaíon   assistance of The Arts Council / An Chomhairle Ealaíon

Front Cover Image: *Concoction* by Alfonso Monreal, 45cmx45cm Oil on Aluminium
Cover design by Brenda Dermody
Set by Siobhán Hutson
Printed by Offset Paperback Mfrs., Inc., PA

'Tá scamall éigin os cionn na hÉireann
Nár fhan dúil i gcéilíocht ag fear ná ag mnaoi;
Ní aithníonn éinne de na daoine a chéile,
Is tá an suan céanna ar gach uile ní.'

Amhrán an Ghorta

For Doireann Ní Bhrian and Jacky Jones

Acknowledgements

Acknowledgements are due to the editors of the following, in which some of these poems have previously appeared:

The Irish Times, *Poetry Ireland Review*, *W.P. Journal*, *The Stinging Fly*, *The Recorder*, *Or Volge l'Anno* (Marco Sonzogni, editor), *Shenandoah*, *The Whoseday Book*, *The White Page/An Bhileog Bhán* and *The Recorder*.

Special thanks to Ciaran Carson for permission to reproduce lines from *Belfast Confetti*.

Contents

III

IV

I

*'… trials and dangers, even so, attended him
even in Ithaca, near those he loved.'*

The Odyssey

The Pearl Sonnet

Now that the donor of it all was dead
she could have it fixed. In the confusion
after the funeral, whether the rope frayed
or was tugged, it broke and all the pearls
were re-strung exactly in the right order – but one.
It had always taken the light differently
irritated the others, not unlike the grain of sand
that was its own conception. Now it was gone.
The necklace glowed, its cool elegance displayed
on public occasions. The missing pearl
was not forgotten – its absence defined how well
the others matched. It was re-set as a pendant.

It hangs at someone else's throat now and looks
well enough, like a tear or an unshed moon.

The Whitethorn Elegy
For J O'Mahony

> *'Angels (it is said) would often be unable to tell*
> *whether they moved among the living or the dead.'*
>   Rilke

This life is raw and raging
and the angels that appear fleetingly are dark.
Over each shoulder and at the foot of the bed –
a large wing rises and – this is a recurring theme –

falls, underneath it down plumps slowly,
rough feathers glint and settle.
They have perched, four rough trade angels
each wing joined to a hod-carrier's shoulder.

I catch a look malevolent as that
of any night-time sailor, but I'm all they've got,
those pirates and roustabouts
ousted in the politics of Heaven, caught

on the losing side – not for them the presidents
and beauty queens but they must be noticed to exist.
They know they are a far cry from the bright
nimbused creatures that were asked for –

the golden boys sent to pillow dreams as light
as the gauze in church paintings over the Christ-child's face.
They stayed back in the dark for years where I only caught
an unthreatening glimpse, in the second before sleep

or the last precipice before waking until once after a night
spent fighting my way out from under a load
of seaweed, one stayed and risked a look of pity,
as if to say he'd had that dream by day.

Then there was the real child
in the dream, the barred bedroom door outside
which he stood calling for his mother – you recognised
the sobbing as your own and held it back – who turned

and limped down the road from the closed door to the sea
afraid of ghosts and birds of prey, one of many
wishing to be loved, he learned the hard way
that some mark or sin had ruled this out.

How you came to know their story, that
some scream and others are beyond screaming because
now only vultures and shades inhabit
their world is the business of Dr. Jung and Dr. Freud

whom you might have hired to banish demons but didn't
– you knew they couldn't shift those bolts an inch – a choice
between Tweedledum and Tweedledee said Mr. Joyce –
all that is academic; the dream is solid as a rock.

ii.

Now I lie me down to sleep, I pray to God my soul to keep.
Mathew, Mark, Luke and John, Bless the bed that I lie on.
Not for us the brief explosion of a star from Heaven.
Those intersections of place and time, where nothing

is black or white exactly and day meets night
briefly before the tireless sun-carrier moves on
the soaring perilous cathedral, the terrible love affair
of Sagrada Familia that we construct

with double vision and half vision
and the architectural retrieval of bad dreams,
is where our fallen angels meet their charges,
children with broken footsteps and club feet,

where they learn to walk without supporting walls
and make do with one another. They swallow
the black caoineadh that once started might never end
and in terror and wonder at this inside-out church, live.

The Abandoned Child

After a photograph by Don Mc Clellan

This is a simple photograph, a black and white picture
of a child lying in the dust. She has no name.
Call her Baby, Beauty, Unbeloved, she is the face of our time.

She is thrown on the earth afraid, abandoned at the limit
of word and note and brushstroke.
Every poem pauses here. Important questions are decided:

Who will feed the child, the price of corn, what happens
to the planets when they die, and how long
do the doomed beauties last with the cameras gone.

The theory holds that a shrunken star will collapse
into a ball so tight, not even light will escape.
Into this invisible hole anything may fall, and has.

As to the children, the books are silent or advise
metaphorical distance. Only the songs remember
the unbreachable chasm between jazz notes,

where dead loves hang. She would be twenty,
maybe twenty-five now, a wife, a washerwoman, a physicist
spreading chaos across the stars. In her alternative Universe

there would be dishes to be washed, children to be
sent to school and minded. She might even now
be writing up a formula on her IBM compatible,

a theorum to predict the trajectory of a mother's kiss.
But in the known world money changed hands. Prisons filled
and the crowd stampeded. She is most likely dead.

She has no name, this beauty lying in the dirt
between well made sonnets and free verse,
without an I or you or us, between the hand's release

and the rattle of the Gorta box. Read her eyes.
The Universe is made up in equal measure of tears
and hunger and bits of string, the old dimensions

and her face has more agony than a medieval Christ.
Her poem is the soundless howl of light streaming
into the black hole of heaven. Trying eternally to get out.

Anniversary

Somewhere between the tight silences, the hard
screaming rows, we have dodged words,
blades aimed to go in deep and wound

and sometimes they have hit, as they say, home,
have gone in and found bone
or worse, poison-tipped, a lobe of lung

or liver. Amazing how with all that going on we
have found time to build a house we like,
rear two children we love but do not always see

and look bewildered when we realise
our almost grown-up son could soon be moving out
with our prayers, but not without our hurts,

as each wonders what damage we have done
and will love ever be enough to make it up to them
and one another. We are still together – amazing

that skiving off from adult duties this afternoon
I find myself astride your hips, our laughter ringing
along the beechwood in our ochre bedroom.

The Dark House

Last night the house pulled open again.
Through the gap in the porch
big enough to let the sky in
I saw a figure on a white horse

riding across the sixpenny moon.
The beams at the gable were
six inches short of their beds
in the wall and the heavy timbered roof

strained apart slowly like a seagull
against a storm. This morning
it was whole again but I know well
they are out there lurking

until the speirbhean sends them pulling
at my shelter. She will not rob me of sleep
but what will happen to the starlings
nesting in the eaves?

On Waking

Something has attracted the wasps
to her new dream.
One has landed and stung
the soft place below her ear.
He is vibrating there,
a stripy drill.
She lacks the courage
to remove him. Is this horror?
Now her throat will close
her tongue swell and the honeycomb
burst in her chest. A swarm
of pliant women will be released.
That's what he's after.

On waking, her fingers survey her throat
and rejoice.
'I am smooth as marble.'
She lies on, basking like an odalisque
in the sweet aftermath of terror.
She dresses slowly and admits her body
a brief perfection, its way with light;
then begins her tasks
amid the chaos of the breakfast table.
It is September and all day long
death buzzes among the apple trees.
When her hand encounters the fruit bowl
her skin prickles
with a furry aftertaste.

The Reckoning

It is the end of another winter
in happy-ever-after land. The glass slipper
pinches and rubs where her feet have swollen
but she tries it on occasionally to please her husband.
She has put aside the dress for her daughter.

Her sisters for reasons best known to themselves
have put her out. When the prince came
not even he could rescue her
from that first eviction, though he tried.
She has only lately understood

it was not his job and that it is useless
to speculate what sin or mark of Cain
made her the one they turned on.
Nor is there any use staring at the lit windows
where the daughters and her mother sit

beside bright fires and talk cosily of trivia
nor into the cafés and hotels
where they convene to lunch and discuss
what? Winter coats, paint, the shape and colour
of new houses, old rooms.

Somewhere along the veins and tributaries
of those meetings, perhaps in the heart's draughty atrium
the order of each child and grandchild is confirmed
according to a sum of family traits proudly
displayed, examined and allowed.

What counts most in this reckoning is
the power of women to leave out unfavoured children.
The crescendo of names not said is like the hiss
of shingle sucked out by an undertow – we all hear it
and are meant to, this silent curse against the unchosen.

Was it worth it, they say, for a dress, a prince,
a glass evening shoe – giving herself airs.
She is used to the boycott. What she cannot bear yet
are the old photographs, the changeling smiles, hers tight
as a drum, theirs open. Silence! The old order ricochets.

The women, their code intact, are superior, ladylike.
To speak would have been a failure of manners,
and ugly. Their silence stills the world, then splinters,
a car bomb primed years ago. Such fuss,
but they don't flinch at news from the North.

Aishling At The Seven Sisters Well

Six statuary women gather
Around the Seven Sisters Well
And one is watching from the ruin
Where roses clot the air.

They pray and circle. Wreaths laid, duty done,
they bask a little
and congratulate each other on their children,
well-turned out, in no doubt of their place
at the hearth. Rite observed,
her marble family leaves. Birdsong resumes.

They go back to their alcoves
satisfied nothing wild will gallop
out of the bushes to disturb their grotto.
Watching from the ruin the seventh
is not so sure. She is looking at the children
for a sign, a double crown or a cow's lick.

Impossible to tell yet in which chest
the scallop of pain is growing –
this circle defines by exclusion.
She sees a tide of hawthorn flow over walls,
the road, houses. It recedes after a deep breath
and a young girl bodysurfs its wake.

The woman leaves her hiding place
in a ruined kitchen.
She makes a cracked bowl of her hands.
The dead pilgrims marvel and place bets
on how often she'll come back to a dry well.
'They are from museums, not churches,'

she tells the girl, her young self
and turns her wet face to the sea
thinking of Odysseus, homesick for all
his journey took from him,
as if the indifferent waves,
ready with comfort or insults, cared.

The Knife God

Tonight, she's breathing stardust.
She'll wake on a bed of golden vowels,
a morphine pump the centre
of her little Universe.
She'll want to please us.
They're all brought down to this –
afraid to ask where we dump the bits.
Oh, we have our embalmers' secrets!
Tomorrow my face will be a monstrance
until the pain hits and she realises.

Deuce

It is time to deal with Death.
We lay our cards on the table,
his hanging man and pentacle
are only a fairground attraction.

We'll play the four honest suits,
my diamonds, his hearts,
my spades to his clubs. Marked, of course.
He has more aces but a few knaves

have found their way into my hand.
I look into his black eyes – yes, afraid.
They hold my stare and he shuffles. Steady.
The stakes are high – the sight of his face:

If I win he will draw back the hood.
His deal, my cut.

.

The Poet's Lover Names Her Price

The week of the Mission in nineteen fifty-nine
a man woke up just as a cat
big as a good-sized dog, sprang.
He was black as the pit of hell
and his eyes were on fire.
A miraculous medal saved the man in the end
but the struggle was terrible.
The smell of burning coal
on flesh and fur, lingered in the room for weeks.
'The claw marks are scrawbed on my back,' he said.

He walks over the roofs
of your slip-slidy dreams.
It is not those modern demons
ineffectual in the light
you should heed –
your nights and your poems
are like suburbs. There is a price
on my love and a reward.

Do something. Perform
a pious or religious act
to attract the big cat.
Grapple the truth from him.
It will take more
than a Latin act of contrition
to break his power
but I will give you an invocation.

Let him once break your stare
and his claws will sink in
to your throat and tear.
He will discard the heart,
it's the soul he's after.
If you win, he'll disappear
leaving the smell of scorched flesh
and a poem. Worth the mess.

The Sky House

The sky house is emptying,
supper guests spilling into the night
calling 'Happy New Year'.
Below us, a late flight disturbing Capricorn
is winking towards America.
Its morse code splashes on the retina
and only these small explosions of light
tell us this is not a star.
Somewhere over the Atlantic
it will collide with last year.

A yellow cat the size of a sheep dog
runs under the streetlights
down an avenue of maroon cypress trees –
but that was in San Francisco, months ago.
There are no street lamps here, nor streets.
I go inside and turn off all the lights but one.
This house lets in the moon from three sides.
My hand reaches into the pool
of the reading lamp and cups a brandy glass.
Beside it, a vase of broom, an open book.

Words are as treacherous as children.
When a poet's voice opens a door
in the night air, there's no knowing
what will be let in – old loves, the yellow cat,
a young killer. I look out and see the glass,
a hand, but no face reflected in the windowpane.
There is a faint blue backlight, like radium.
Signals, from God knows where in the Nebula
are passing through me, encoding bone
and tissue with messages for transcription or translation.

Down from the gable, the shades are back,
ploughing by moonlight. Their stumpy horses
are kept hidden by day on the islands
and the hungry dead, buried upright
are out on unfinished business.
A voice, closer than blood says
'Sometimes it's best to follow the poem.'
The plane, invisible now, cuts its silent track
through sable – the stars have gone in.
I toast the moon, a cold nun, and the sky shuts.

After The Funeral, The Departure

The bags are badly packed, is a last look allowed?
Before I leave I'll dust the lovely perfume flasks and wrap them
in a silk scarf like metaphors or torahs, storm green, chalice red
and a gold flecked cobalt I bought in Israel.

They have survived the rock splitting under the house,
the walls straining like weightlifters' arms, the noise.
I have seen objects as delicate in a New York museum,
a pretty Etruscan amphora beside some Spartan vases.

Time to roll up my sleeves, there is domestic work
waiting – knives to be sharpened, the house scoured, a grave
to be dug. Even if I am incompetent and hear the tough
women laughing at my efforts, see the disgust carved

into their faces as I sit with my forehead on the foot
of a sunken grave, let them be disgusted. I am disgusted myself.
I didn't see it boomeranging back to the weak spots until it hit –
the ga bolga in the heart, the eye, the right breast.

All that remains is to let the wind read each face accurately –
to say goodbye lightly would be nice but I do not;
I move on reluctantly, like every daughter of history
who has left her father's house unwillingly or late.

II

In the Name of God and
of the Dead Generations

I will tell you the sound the wounded make.
First let this be clear:
I always knew what belonged to me.
The piece of ground under my feet
or my sleeping body was mine
and all the land between
an imaginary line fifteen feet
above the high water mark
and the shore at low tide,
not including Manhattan
and in Spring, more,

which might be why Mediterranean
coastal regions pulled me
with their small tides,
or areas of high seismic activity
such as Lisbon and San Francisco,
so much for place. Yes
it has mattered, yes we replace
rock with the shimmering space
an idea of a rock where the rock has been.

Yes, I understand abstraction.
It is the welcoming place
into which strangers may come,
people with gypsy blood and skin
darker again than that
of certain fishermen along the coast
but that all said I was born outside the pale
and am outside it still. I do not fit in.

Let me tell you the sound the wounded make.
Vowels that rise out of slashed throats
will be somewhat strangled
and inelegant in our Hiberno English –
the gurgled speech of Kosovo
ringed with hard Dublin argot
from the inner city
or drawn out by tender vowels in Clare
sounds uneducated as well as broken.
This is not sexy English,
not the accent to elicit
'Put a bit of butter on the spuds Andre.'

There were new Jews in Brooklyn, new Irish
in the Bronx a hundred years ago –
their 'sweedhard' and 'stoah'
unbecoming in the mouths of young men
from Carna or Warsaw. These are the sounds
the wounded make.
An old man from the Gaeltacht at a wedding
'Excuse me, miss, I don't speak English so good',
the Miss a branding iron.
In Irish the sentence would have sung.

We have spent a small ransom
remembering the famine
that some of us never forgot
in Universities all over America
and never gone looking for the ones that got away
from Mother Machree and the ancient order
of Hibernians, the black Irish.
They left in the darkened holds of coffin ships,
they arrive sealed in the holds of containers
wounded, sometimes dead, between the jigs and the reels
and the Céad Míle Fáilte.

Violation

'I'd twist it inside out, this coil that led me on and on, and brings me back
To the red bud of his buttonhole, a shower of red confetti.

'Or to this scenario of her as Wolf, and me as Little Red Riding Hood
Being gobbled up...'

Ciaran Carson, *Belfast Confetti*

Blue grass can still be bought and so can 'Le Must
du Cartier' in case you thought to ask
later in a different poem and 'Je Reviens'
can still be sung.

This country of ours is violent
I think to myself this morning with surprise –
I only lately realised that dancehall fights
were not as usual everywhere, nor everywhere excused
as young men going wild. I mean in Connemara, not Belfast.
Half-murdering your neighbour at a dance
at Christmas and St. Patrick's Day
was not, it seems, considered de riguer
for young men everywhere but there it is:

Women of good breeding in the West
retired after a good look from balcony or chair
to the toilets to repair the damage caused by sweat, fear
and excitement, as etiquette demanded.

I never understood the impulse to pulverise flesh
with bricks or bats but – let's stick
to what we know – an arc just like a reaping hook and deep
opens across a dancer's cheek, stops just below the eye,
follows a neighbour's practiced crack, the whiskey bottle
smashed across a bench, and – 'Say that again you bastard.'

This tableau surprised but did not shock.
Later I found the jagged weapon on the floor
marked 'Paddy' like an English joke.

Those men had wives at home, and daughters,
were kind to me, respectful always.
We were schooled in such accommodations
as women made with men's natures. Why is it then
I see the drops of blood like garnet beads
before a watery liquid joined the dots,
my neighbour's eyes, feral, nothing familiar there but lust;
why when history's black hags dive into our personal sky
at inappropriate times, the woods are full of hump-backed beasts
and all the lovely dancing girls emerge
from Kosovo and Africa and places around here
with their giggling dreams in rags around their breasts.

Fate

After Caitlin Maud

If this rusted petal could moisten and tint
I'd have a hundred blinded girls

weave a silk carpet for your feet. You'd walk
in here and gossip for hours, sitting cross-legged.

If it could find its way back
even to the original rose

your footsteps would still blaze
out across the world.

You would leave your lover's bed refreshed
and come home to sleep in his arms.

But no. The hawthorn has stopped
in mid flowering, as if recalled

and you, Caitlin, will stay
the dark side of the glass, a watcher.

This petal will not find a place
among her rustling sisters.

It too will remain what it is:
a memento mori, like all love tokens.

Irish

It didn't, you see, die back.
It was hacked.

Regaining ground
it has lost foliage.

We can live without
the full savour

of the moon's vowels
but what about the howl

of loss? Still, some songs
will wait for the right singer.

Area of Scientific Interest

On my first visit after the solstice,
delayed by a good storm,
the woman in the stone house spoke:
'I will rise and drink the morning
even this grey daylight
that is neither sunny nor beautiful
but stuck like a half-torn rag
on a holly bush, a plastic bag in a doorway
at the fag end of the century,' she greeted me.

'I will rise and eat the black clouds
that stick in my craw
because they are merciful and hide
the bloody necklaces of Kosovo,
the planes over Baghdad,
the cold faces of the subsidy-checkers in Dublin,
stemming what comes in on the tide
not knowing that flotsam and jetsam
is what keeps coastal people going. But I tell you,'
she said, 'they have lives of pure misery.
Such misery as you never saw –

halfpence and pence.'
She got up and took in gulps
of bad weather and dressed herself in tattered clouds
magnificent in her own way. Then we breakfasted.
She poured tea into elegant cups.
'I always liked fine china,'
and the fire reddened in the grate
and we ate the bad morning and it did us no harm.
'We'd make great queens,' she remarked,
'Or a damned sight better than what's there.'
We looked out over the waves. 'A big sea.'
She made an elegant arc of her arm, trailing cumulii.

'That is an Area of Scientific Interest
according to Brussels.'
'Did you ever meet a bureaucrat?'
She asked as if I might have unwittingly entertained
one in my home,
his pointy hooves hidden in patent leather shoes,
they being practiced in the art of surprise.
'Talking golf-sticks, most of them.
They wouldn't care if I was ten miles out past Slyne Head
clinging to a barrel so damn their souls to hell.'
We drank our Barry's tea.
Charity may be all very well for those
that lie on under the covers on cold mornings
but not for women in stone houses
at the edge of the sea.

The Heroine of the Western World

I tried everything, your honour
but in the end I was driven to it –
I went to a cailleach first.
Get a priest, she told me.
Tell him you have nightmares.
Ask him to exorcise them.
Tell him there are all sorts of people
escaping from your husband's dreams into yours.
There are some things a wife
doesn't want to know.
If he refuses, give him a good flaking
with a sweet sea rod – not too thick –
he'll soon agree – priesteens are soft.

But no, my husband wouldn't have it.
No priest is going to come between
me and my wife before God,' he said.
'Right so,' I said. 'Have it your way.'
And he did. No fault divorce.
The divorce I want has plenty of fault,
most of it his.

Not all, mind you. He did the dishes.
Though he wasn't what you might call tasty.
But what got me was the dreams –
the goings on and nothing much going on
if you see what I mean. Pure havoc.
Then there was the fear that my own dreams
might leak – that was the mental torture.
Which brings us to the poker, the split skull.
Not what we class serious around here.
Sure he was bound to recover.
After a suitable lapse for the plot
to develop. This being the West.

The Republic of Acronyms

In the Republic of Acronyms
everything is a synonym for money.
The Regional Hospital Galway
changed its name to UCHG,
out with the old, in with the new acronym
for 'Put your money where your bypass is'
and Guinness Book of Record waiting lists
or even 'Go home and die roaring' in Latin.
And that's only in English –
they need Irish for funding
new logos with half the alphabet
tortured into queer shapes.
But the dual language version
is a sight. Unseen.
Logo, Greek for word. For reason.

Every institution of learning is merging
with some corporation, selling themselves
like that old whore commerce
to the bidder with the longest acronym.
There will soon be no-one left to advise
on pronunciation – whether an unvoiced G
is permissable and what to do
with four hefty consonants in a row
or three grouped threateningly
around a slim vowel. Growling.

In the matter of rhyming – GMIT
(the old Regional Tech)
best works with vomit but that brings us back
to UCHG and the queue in Casualty. Or gromet.
And makes the hospital sounds like a dog
getting sick. Violently.

Or a people Gulliver met and thought polite
not to mention out of consideration to our soft palates.

'I reached the land where the Ukhig dwelt'.
Or 'The Ushig, a sibilant people with pointy heads
rowed out to greet me in little black coracles...'
We could rhyme Ushig with brostig in Kerry Irish
and go stark raving macaronic but that sets
a dangerous precedent in a town where the University
answers to the name of NUIG.

The Ballad of Pepsi and Wonderbra

Mr. Diet Coke met Miss Wonderbra
whose legs are in the Guinness Book of Records
– for length – on mid-morning radio.
'Hello,' he said, 'so you're in Dublin.
I'm in Dublin too. Let's meet' and then
they swapped vital statistics on the air.
She started it. 'How tall are you?' she asked.
When he said her bosom would be in line with his...
'Hey guys, the line is live.'
The would-be shock jock tried to get back
into the conversation
he had started with salacious
talk of bosoms, thighs, the hard job
of finding a woman to equal Mr. Coke or Pepsi's
charms. He had only recently been saved
from being torn apart on that very same show
by secretaries driven mad with lust.
It seems he has the secretaries of Ireland
baying at the moon with desire which confirms
my suspicion of office work.

'She can't cook,' the presenter said, as if cooking
was a dirty word. She giggled and quickly passed
to talk of uplift. I thought there was a lot to be said
for certain Latin American books on the culinary arts,
even Calvino's thoughts on chilis, but decided
this was not the time to phone in. I also wondered
what legs had to do with it and wasn't she wasted on a bra
and did she double job for Pretty Polly.
Then there were his legs, which got no airing.
That's hardly gender equality, now is it?
'We'll talk to you nearer your destination,'
the presenter said to remind her she was on a job.

'Oh yeah,' she said, 'whatever,' and resumed
the real conversation until he cut them off.
I hate when they do that.
Now we'll never know his height.

Committed

The woman in the bed
in the hospital for the mad
in Ballinasloe shrivelled
under a thin blanket.
'May the curse of Almighty God
burn the ground from under
that lightening bitch' –
the nurse that reported
'No improvement' to the doctor.
Then her voice collapsed
in on itself like a tent.
'Ask them to get me out,' she said,
'Tell them to bring me home' –
her eight grown children.

The visitor was young and frail
in that department herself.
She spent the next ten years afraid
of the guard, a parent,
a doctor with a pen gathered
to commit her. The sin was fear
of the dark, the Blessed Mother's eyes
following her, being left alone
with the replay of a ruined voice
winding down.
At the end of a decade
she packed her black
lace mantilla and went to Spain,
found a lover with soft eyes,
was able to ignore
the tortured Jesus statues
that celebrate death –
this was suffering worth
going to Heaven for.

Best of all she made a home
in their language. The words
quickened her tongue.
She told the trees
in Seville her story. She was free
from the statues' fish eyes
until she remembered Lowry Loinseach
and his ass's ears. She heard her secret
whispered over the breakfast marmalade.
The women's smiles jacknifed,
their lips snapped closed
like purses. Now the oranges growing
along the sidewalks
reminded her of hospitals.
After the glorious mysteries
the sorrowful.

The Second Plantation of Connaught

Do Scriobhnóiri Inis Mór

'We love Connemara. Bought a little place there.
It's paradise,' the woman brays, adjusting
her children like accessories.
Even Cromwell knew better.
Failed the first time. Scraggy blackthorn
not covering the rock's shame, the soil
taken to Aran as a joke. To hell
was the alternative, a hell without golf,
decent restaurants or friends from Blackrock.
Now they come to play, copper-fingered
as that old snob Yeats predicted.

The failed Gaels, set-dancing to save our souls
talk the talk and walk the quickstep.
They have claimed Irish
as their territory, staked it out,
are dug in like sappers.
They know what is good for us and do not
keep wisdom to themselves.
We know them by the labels on their new coats,
their bainín jackets – Jimmy becomes Seamus,
Mike turns into Micheal overnight.

The locals, sure of what they are
do the opposite. They listen to country music,
speak Irish on the mobile, misbehave
linguistically.
'Connemara Rock, a deir sé. No hassle.'
This place is too small
to bear the weight of everybody's dreams
which failing, turn. Snarling. It matters

that we pave our own roads once,
just once in all of history be our own surveyors.

I keep faith with the faithless tribes
as best I can:
Ó'Direáin, Ó' Flatharta, Ó Cadhain, Caitlín Geal,
and see them driven out, one by one.

Cargo de Nuit
i.m. Anne Kennedy

Driving from Claremorris, where a poet's lost love —
that great love certain men excel in and are always losing —
provided a brief respite from compulsory revelry,
I kept vigil for a dying actor,
imagined his retreat into that last cathedral silence,
his snow-is-general-all-over-Ireland vowels stilled
in the ante-chamber of expected death.
I drove into organised mayhem, public noise.

I was saying Kaddish for Allen Ginsberg
in a Catholic way, chanting the Molluch section
at Galway, when suddenly in a bookshop
your face was before me. It was as if
you had walked in and spoken.

There was too much distance between near spaces.
That night, hearing that a boy,
a shepherd like the young Giotto
had drowned slaking his thirst in a bog lake,
the exploding town with its ersatz demons
sent me cartwheeling back into the real dark.

Your black and white apparition
anchored me among the fireworks, the gaudy stars
exploded harmlessly and cathedral walls parted
to let in the ordinary night. You said:
'That all the bereaved may become Buddhists
or believers in the glorious mysteries
When they wake in the black light.'

My Mac

I was in Dun Eochaill when lightening struck
my Apple Mac and roasted its little modem.
I stepped outside the prehistoric fort
summoned on the mobile phone
to watch the thunder heading towards me
– a pathetic fallacy, I know but one I'm fond of.
'It's happened again,' he said.

We bought a PC. It sits in the nook, gaudy and vulgar
like a trophy wife. Fit for soccer and
turning tricks, trying to get us interactive.
I hate it like poison. I don't want to interact
with my dictionary, nor yet a thesaurus.

Now when I go into my room and turn on my modest
long-suffering machine, an electronic pen, nay quill,
I sit thinking how like a blank white page
the screen is, how still and unassuming the little icon.
The apple in the top left hand corner will become
the first decorated letter on a saint's vellum if this goes on
much longer. Why can't the people who made
the atom bomb fix this? Why do I have to sit looking
at burnt offerings, asking what attracts lightning. Twice.

Cleo

She was a six month Spring in a dark year.
We were waiting for fine weather
to take her swimming, nervous
she'd destroy Trá Mhór with her enthusiasm
for digging. She was everything she could be,
hoovering up smells from the kitchen floor.
Silvery pink, klutzy one minute,
a hound of heaven the next, all she. Lovely Cleo.

Angry Arthur
For Maeve

He sat on his bed in a rage that grew
like a thundercloud and ripped its electrical
discharges across the sky and into the earth
where it caused such tectonic havoc –
a subterranean clatter of dishes –
that the house shook, the planet tore apart
and Arthur was left on a raft of rock out in space
lamenting his temper.
                  For years
it was your favourite book and when
every door in the house banged, the walls shook,
and we said 'Forget the damned dishes so'
and you stomped upstairs, leaving the dog
covering his eyes in relief, the air shivering
in your wake and the proper parenting guide
In flitters at our feet
                you always lay
on your duvet covered raft, way beyond us.
'I'm not sorry,' you'd shout and I screamed back
'See if I care,' because at those times
I was only your own age and afraid
you would stay out there
in your lonely orbit and leave us forever
because we had been bad.

Anubis In Oghery

For Oisin

Our dog, Georgie is dead. She lived
with us for ten years and walked three miles a day
with me but loved you best because she was
mostly yours. Now I have to watch your face
the reddening look, as if it might break open
and think there is something about a man's pain
that cracks like chestnuts or old timber.
It is not lubricated by tears.

You buried her down among the hazels
and blackberries, made a cairn on the grave
planted two birch trees. No-one instructed you
in these rites. Yesterday you were a small boy
playing with a pup that chewed windows. Now
you walk away, a dream dog at your heel. Tall, able.

III

The Cost of the Gift

He mortified the flesh, she pampered it. She mocked,
he shook his big head. She thought he was her bedrock.
When he moved, he took the ground out from under her.
That's how we believe it was because a woman

that loves with desperation goes mad when her house
breaks. The pain of those seams parting slowly between
roof and wall is more than she can bear this morning.
He strides away with his head in Ursa Major.

At home in the Universe, he's breathing free air.
She sees the house Gods leaving, like pets in his wake.
Sparks break off the stars and fly to his anvil chest,
ash settles on the sofa, on the children's beds.

When he pitches his tent out beyond Sirius
she's stuck in the house. In such a situation
one way or another, one often dies: people
take sides, the laws of mourning are not well observed.

What of him, recalled to a cold hearth, the beauty
evicted and his ribcage straining like roofbeams –
did the household Gods sneak back like appalled children
and did he pet them absently because it was

not their fault? Neither the marble statues nor the
earthenware head. All speculation but two things:
his dark familiars, crow, jaguar, fox, though loosed, stayed;
from that day out, one eye, the hunter's, never slept.

The Joiner's Bench

Somehow she found herself drawn
to his desk, that intimate place,
ran her hand over its surface
as you would smooth a skirt down.
A ridge where the lathe skipped
delayed her and she looked up at his eyes
surprised how familiar
their blue black stain. It spread like ink.

His mind played over her poems,
her hand slipped over the scarred timber,
a wave of slim-fingered elegance. Best left at this
best to have set the ocean on fire
between them than a shared desk —
trees were her nemesis.

Birthday Gift

She was selfish, a total bitch
with her perfume and elegant wounds.
He was a complete bastard,
useless in her pain, trapped, the way a man is:
fox smell, fox soul. With one all positive,
the other all negative
and those great bolts of attraction
there was bound to be overload. He ran from her noise,
her painted hearts screaming 'Love me, Love me'.
Like lipsticked mouths.

In all that English wasteland
his retreat into dens and sets
was protective colouring to stave off savage gods.
The gift, that it didn't work.

The Poet's Fancy

The moment the long stride
is heard across the countryside
the bush telegraph of otter,
badger, thrush flashes the message.
'Quick lads, run, scatter, dive.
It's the poet.' They're afraid of their lives
where they'll end up –
in a trap, at the end of a hook
or dead on some godforsaken road
in the west of Ireland,
their little paws raised for all to pity.

Either that or having sex
in trees, pools, nests, anywhere but beds
with the entire cast of the Faber Book of Beasts
looking on – poets have no sense of decency.
They could even lose their pelts,
skins, feathers.
By the time his shadow falls across the river
the only thing to greet the poet's eager look
is the swirl of a disappearing tail
and the hush of a thousand thrushes
holding their breath. The badger,
knowing what he knows, has long gone.

The Blue Cat

See how magnificently he lies.
Any minute now
he will step across the kitchen tiles

and brush against your bare ankles
with all that fur on skin implies.
Be fooled. Take what comfort you can.

He too suffers from some vast loneliness.
His family ties are as tenuous
as yours. Those god-green eyes

are crystals mined from deep in the pit.
They condemn him to night combat,
dawn raids. It is not his fault

that the vase is broken. He can not go back.
In the morning as you face the mirror
to decipher the night's havoc

when the cries that stabbed last night's dream
swirl like dirty water
into the vortex of your cat-green eyes, pity him.

The Fox and The Hare

It is November and all September's stillborn
poems are buried under the ferns
or choked by thorns. Soon the back-garden briars
will have died back, the green filigree
rotted, leaving a rusted tracery,
then we will see where we stand;
either their sad skeletons or the shapes,
each absence muscular and defined
where hare and fox, the reliable Gods
of sinew and trickery, have lain and fled.

All this time I have been lighting small fires,
my breath coaxing the home embers
each morning and my nights, the long nights
feeding the monster in the stars.

Research & Development

It works like this: an unsuspecting family
normal in most ways are expecting a baby
or perhaps it's already arrived (the trauma is worst
for the parents in the case of the eldest).
There are no early signs, nothing to indicate
it might be better left in a draught
though a lot of them are delicate
and tend to get TB, asthma, trouble with breath –
it might be worth investigating lungs –
but generally all seems well until adolescence
when the first symptoms appear:
arguments, strange clothes, an awkward manner
though nothing as clear as mumbling in verse
or scanning the milk carton, nothing obvious.
It's a blow to any family and theories vary
as to whether society's to blame or destiny.
Some say it barrels down the DNA chain
from some ancestor, like a recessive gene –
in which case there's hope we could identify
the coding and eliminate the rogue activity
that for years lies dormant but in wait
to turn a normal healthy person poet.

Afternoon Tea and Quoof

After a month of hard graft and the train
journey to Dublin in the inevitable rain
to discuss poems with students in Trinity,
poems that include strange sounding words
and the spoor of the Yeti,
and wondering not for the first time about the girl
around whose breast the poet's hand curls,
(not least wondering if this is the kind of good works
a mother-of-two should be doing in the name of poetry);
it is not expedient to have afternoon tea
in the Shelbourne, with green
watered silk wall-covering and high ceilings,
and spoon cream over the jam on our scones.

As we travel lightly, I might even say with indolence
from Donegal to San Francisco and New York
troubles fade and questions such as what
was the poet's hand doing on the girl's breast
and a hot water bottle between them in the bed
recede. Afternoon tea is not expedient but it helps.

The Loose Alexandrines

Shameless they parade twelve by twelve by twelve across
the pages out of uniform. They wear high heels
one with dyed blonde hair has a run in her stockings
and another of very unresolved gender

though I predict he will have a feminine end
and it serves him right – is dancing over the line
dressed in leather pants with a big star on his crotch.
It lights up – now what do you think he got that for?

Not his prosody. Look what happens as soon as
you relax the rules. First they make up their own. Soon
they're stravaiging over the pages in loose ranks
total anarchy – where's the poetry in that?

Muck savages, socialists, up from the country,
I disapprove of the regions and those people
without so much as a degree from Trinity,
with relations in Boston instead of Blackpool

marching out with the best of us. The Atlantic!
The poetic equivalent of red lipstick.
Books must be prescribed – more Larkin, less Yeats, no Plath,
no mad women – you're safe with Bishop and Clampitt.

Poetry must be strict and purge itself to survive.
It's time to round them up and herd them, twelve by twelve
by twelve into sheep pens, the lads divided from
the girls, the pigs from the pearls, the boys from the men.

Blaithín

She was ready to bud
when the fire-king found her.
Though a God,
he was the devil of a lover.
At each lick a bloom
of red or orange opened –
Mont Bretia, peony, rose –
until she was all flowers.
'Petal,' he whispered when he bedded her.
How she flamed.
Then, his pleasure taken, he left her
burning like a garden in hell.

Advice

It seems to me, love
despite fashion and decadence
a girl needs to know where she stands.
But there's no use asking
men don't suit introspection,
it confuses them. They rarely
grasp the most glaring implications
behind questions put
in perfectly simple English.
And when feeling trapped, will hide
behind the monosyllables. So

I have devised a test.
Put him to work on the long grass –
it's a jungle down there below the willows –
and hide the lawnmower.
Hand him a scythe.
You'll soon know if he's limp-wristed.
It isn't sexual stereotyping,
men are good at this kind of thing.
It stops them beating you up and complaining
and they have the build for it
or ought to.

I know you say you're not the marrying kind
but let me show you how to make
a sinful, if passé, chocolate roulade –
in other words, log. Look, Diana,
a girl should have one good culinary skill,
though I think I agree,
you are more suited to the bow and arrow.

Wanted, Muse

Are you young, female with long legs?
Mysterious eyes, any colour
but the blacker the better,
Rosaleen. Degree optional though it is

essential to be literate – you'll be required
to read the poet's work, to distinguish
his gifts from his attributes – analysis
won't be necessary. A nice smile, for 'she smiled'

and a tendency to appear shrouded in mist
early in the morning, but only when
accompanying the poet on his visits
to the country – aishlingí are passé in the town.

Blonde is good, dark preferred
love of cheap wine and travel combined
with a talent for exciting writing lust
is vital. As for the hair, dye if you must.

Are you young, male, with long legs and bi-
lingual skills? Poetry is an equal opportunity employer.
Gardening and good biceps are a priority.
Sigh if you must, but remember, poets value muscularity.

Ceres in Caherlistrane

For Colum McCann

Somewhere near forty second street
a girl, copper-haired, sings for a hawk-eyed man.
He tastes, in the lark's pillar of sound
honey and turf-fires. A tinker's curse rings out:

this is the voice of Ireland, of what we were.
He approves. Her hair gleams. There is a vow.
Later, she skips into the graffiti-sprayed subway.
At the edge of hearing, a laugh, a man's death cry,

a woman's love call are carried out of the tunnel's
round mouth caught in the snatch of a tune
she has no idea these underriver walls
are shored up with Irish bones, black men's bodies.

She thinks all the buskers in New York are down
here tonight like cats. She hears them – a keen,
a skein of blues. They speed her passage. She hums,
picking up the echoes in her riverrun.

In Galway, her stooked hair ripens that Summer.
At Hallowe'en there are wine apples. A seed caught
in her teeth will keep the cleft between this world
and the next open, the all souls' chorus a filter

for certain songs that rise from a cold source.
Brandy and honey notes replace spring water –
the gift price to sing an octave deeper
than sweet, tuned to a buried watercourse.

★ *Wine apple is another name for the pomegranate.*

Drowsy Maggie

They call me Drowsy Maggie for the look in my eye
and the hitch of my Fenian red skirt on my thigh.

The women that hate me are wrong to complain,
I keep secrets their bedrooms could never contain.

If I'm free with my favours I'm no soldier doll,
I'm a patriot, with many an explosive wee story to tell

though I mix, with permission and sing a wild song
about love and conscription to boys far from home

I coax the secrets from their mouths, sweets from a child.
They court and win me with little offerings of words.

Women despise me but they owe me their men.
Because of me they sleep safe in their green beds. Sin

lies in the mouth of a gun, in the silencing
of a good reel. Listen, there's a fiddle tuning

a quick-step to see that off-key rebel songster out –
in matters of timing I'm as quick as a shot.

Calliope House Quadrille

The lights are all lit in Calliope House, is the family dining?
The horses smile and the merry-go-round
is ready and turning. The set is painted and the cameras rolling.
Who will get on? Over the water in an octagon room
the whistles are blowing.
Up in the castle the fiddles are tuning. And the fifes and the drums.

Who will come courting the thin daughter sullen as the moon?
Éire waits for the young men. As each one approaches
a red carnation unfurls on his breast.
She plucks it to set off her green wedding dress.

In her heart are the words of a horsewoman's curse
but 'There's no business like showbusiness,' she sings, in Irish.

Captain Roque

'Do you remember how we met?'
he asked me yesterday. I'm not likely to forget,
his sword at my throat. Toledo steel,
and he was damn good but a pitch of the caravelle
turned the tables. Lover, do you remember that
and the storm-tossed nights?

I'm not a woman to weaken for love
but I'd give all except the lives of my men to forgive
his attempted mutiny.
I'd say his hands pirated the garnet at my throat
the dreams from my pillow and nothing else,
but coming from a house of pirate women
I'll call him captain of his own shipwreck
and mine, like he called me his sea queen.

The Spanish Lady

What, you ask, made me want to get away?
Things that happened. Or didn't – you know how it is.
A dream of wrecked ships across the moon,
the belief, growing into certainty, that I was born
in Fuento Vaqueros in Southern Spain.
Years later, when an old man handed me
a red carnation in the Grenada sun
I knew I had followed the right dream.

Have no fear I will forget the quotidian,
your beloved particular. Who could imagine
the effect of oranges on a child reared on rock;
what desire is squeezed into her thin hand
reaching for the home-from-hospital fruit,
the fire in those small dimpled suns?

IV

'Nights full of green stars from Ireland,
Wet out of the sea, and luminously wet,
Like beautiful and abandoned refugees.

The whole habit of the mind is changed by them...'
Wallace Stevens

These Are Not Sweet Girls

'After every war
Someone has to tidy up.'
  Wislawa Szymborska

The wounds women inflict softly on women
are worse than any lover can do
because they are more accurate. Such women
lead from behind silence. They are Ophelia's big sisters
the marrying kind, their power, mediated through men.
Their smiles hook around rivals' throats
like necklaces. They are sweet in company.

Then there are women who undersand the night,
those who have read the wind correctly and know
the real business of the world
could be decided by women alone
and be better managed – but want men
for their honest lies, a door held open, a thorny rose:
they are always promising something.

I myself am happy to barter the well-run shop
for sweet rain, a hand steadying my shoulder
like a wave.
Only this morning a man's mercury shadow
ran through my fingers when I woke.
He drained through my sleep. For hours
I heard a voice in the upstairs rooms – echo, echo.

Such men are first principles – they represent themselves
poetry, lust. They lie with honesty that women lack
and take our breath away with masterpieces,
like Rodin's stolen kisses or the portraits
of Picasso's mistresses, one after another.
Somewhere between their eyes and the wine
we recognise need and admit the honest truth:

These are the world's great lovers,
the men who like women.
Such a man will write one hundred love poems
to wife number three
and she will let herself be taken in. Such a man   ·
causes sensible woman to wear high heels,
skirts, hearts on our silk blouses like statues.

We pay attention briefly to our own desires
over the wants of our children
who orbit us like small moons – this is why we love them.
You Latin women are not fooled.
When he leaves you say: 'Such bastards.'
And 'Love has done this to me'
as if love happens to women

governing them like a verb, or the moon.
You laugh at his photograph appearing
in a bookshop six thousand miles away
as if that was the least he could do, you both
being Catholic. Apparitions of lovers
are commonplace in South America. Here, it's saints.
You are not nice girls.

In the face of cancer and betrayal you open the whiskey
smoke cigars and kick off your shoes.
This is the real constituency of women
where it is not enough to sweep up the mess
when unspeakable things are done
to your children. You insist
there has to be singing, a dance in the face of death.

---

* *These Are Not Sweet Girls*, Poetry by Latin American Women
(New York, White Wine Press)

Diego Ruined Frida Kahlo

She loved him.
How did it happen?
A look between them,
his fingers slipping down her dress
smoothing the cotton.
She was forewarned about artists and pain
but this was different, no choice.

Opening the Anthology of Latin
American Poetry a voice
barely audible, mentions in my ear
that there is an icy feel to the air.
Autumn, the second that year
his gift to me.
Crisp as a glass of dry white wine.
Diego ruined Frida Kahlo
or she him.

Pretty Pussy

This is a well brought up girl.
She sits, her paws daintily together
and greets her master
with pink tongued mews of pleasure,
but she's all cat
when the moon comes out –
her eyes turn to slits of green desire.
She watches him as she sits,
intent on his giblets.

The Red Cat

She went missing the night
I saw Frida Kahlo's ghost crying for Diego,
beautiful Fa Fa, our strawberry blonde cat
fey as the Brazilian torch singer we named her for.
We suspected the neighbours
of seducing her with juicy chicken
or that the odd surreptitious kick and general ill will
from the males in the house had finally driven her out.
We were frantic women with vivid imaginations.

I shut the library door, opened a book –
muscular North of England tom cats sprang out at me,
and turned away, bored. My stomach clenched –
your flourescent pink swimsuit missing from a beach
outside Lisbon when you were two dazzled me.
Then you came bursting in shouting 'Look who's here'
and lifted her head to my forehead to be rubbed.
We made a fuss of her wet red fur,
glad to have her back, our foxy cat, prodigal, well-loved.

We were happier now than before.
Her soft presence pervaded the house for hours,
in direct proportion to the brief calamity of her absence.

At Six p.m.

We are converging on the night's
diamond opportunity.
The moon glows like a host
from within. It has risen early
this September night, for us. Soon
all this promise will ignite
fire in your eyes, or be gone

but now it is stretched between us
this sacramental moment
like a web, whose dewdrops
glitter when some warm
nocturnal animal, perhaps a fox,
senses your approach
and shivers in the bushes.

A Question of Travel

'Continent, city, country, society:
the choice is never wide and never free.'
   Elizabeth Bishop

A man and a woman left a pleasant party
after dinner in the Berkeley hills.
As they stepped off the pavement
on an ordinary street
the night sheathed its claws,
pink and purple blossoms stood out
inches from their stalks,
their electric light glowing.
Their hosts' house silenced behind them,
a moon shone and the breathable surface of the air
was faintly iced.

The man, in shadow, spoke softly.
'This, the wine and the curve of the Pacific
is enough.'

She thought
'I have lived at the edge of volcanic faults
before. The possibility of fire under my feet
suits me – this narrow crust fools no-one.'
Virgil might be wandering below them
with Dante lying on his breast,
looking for the head-centaur's advice.
She is not afraid at all.
Neither shade's feet will disturb a loose stone
wherever they are walking now.

She remembered an October day in Roundstone
stepping out of her car
onto a trawler and out the bay
where a hundred dolphins played
their great circle, how she saw her children
backflipping down the double helix of DNA
to a pink city, their faded crucible twice through fire
and each time rebuilt; saw them
in her mind's eye swoop down
from Castelo Sao Jorge into the Tagus
and out the faulted bay towards Africa
towards life.

'There were four hundred English speakers
in all of California in 1841.' *She was not surprised*
to read this months later, had known it
for a place where more went on
between the tongue and soft palate
than the Declaration of Independence.
This was a giant's land and the city
built on his haunch, shoulder,
in the curve of his waist
knows it is blessed. It knows that one day
he will stretch and there will be burning in Paradise.

She thinks the boy Giotto herds his sheep
below on Angel Island. She is still,
perhaps for the first time, and safe.
Here is a base note she might touch again
and does. It comes back at times
of such midnight pain that her breath
is an hour glass contraction
and she swims up the dolphins ampersand
as if giving birth to herself, then glides down
on a bell's clear vibrato.

Perhaps far above them a growl
really lifted out of the pit, a pack
of untamed gutterals streamed out
across the bay and it was this lightning
that funnelled down her spine
like a flare from Charlie Parker's saxophone
and earthed – certainly he could
with promises like poems
have coaxed the last wild cat
in the hills above San Francisco down
to a clearing under the eucalyptus trees
but they stood among the kissing
and hugging of departing guests
and did not touch once as the air
around them crisped and burned.

From Moycullen to Annaghmakerrig

The sun rising, the guts of an animal,
the town rising, a crow feasting.
The last of the sea. Muck spreaders.
A young woman made up fully
at 7.30 a.m. in a fast car.
A hedge shaped like a tap.
The Blessed Virgin in the clouds.
A moot with daffodils. Cows.
A man in a green jaguar and shades.

An old woman with a fierce face.
The Bog Lane Theatre where
you could take a wrong turn.
The churches growing more Protestant
towards Cavan. Bad signposting
in Edgeworthstown. Potholes, a man
that looks like a killer of women in cars
following me for miles outside Edgeworthstown.
Wrong directions to Newbliss.

The accents changing,
right directions to Newbliss.
Designer bullet holes
in the Annaghmakerrig sign.
Very Monaghan. The boreen, the gates,
the house. All comforting.
Then red blossoms like Cordoba at Easter.
They are, the Gardener says,
only rhododendrons.

The Stone Nymph

For Frankie McDonagh

I went to visit a friend
and found her like God in goggles
carving a woman out of rock,
a roundy thighed female
stretched out in her sandstone pelt.
The sculptor was dressing her hair
with a chisel and mallet.

She rolled lazily out of the stone,
a young strap, beyond control already.
She smiled through the grainy dust
as if Jove himself had just left her.
The look on the artist's face was saying
in nine months time, my lady
you'll get your comeuppence.

Macchu Picchu, Inis Mór

For Pura Lopez Colome

On the ferry out we talk about marvels:
the poet that left his mistress for his wife –
and translate images; they break the surface
of our talk like new islands. To the west
a red heart bleeds over the airstrip,
to the east, licked by terra cotta flames
a daz-white angel is fighting the devil for a soul –
he pulls desperately on one leg
but the devil has him by the head. The soul
scorched and nearly torn in two
is wearing a bainín jacket and Reebok trainers –

it must be the Gaeltacht they're intent on saving.
The soul is hacking at them both
with a rusty halo bent into a T na G logo.
What would that mean in Mexico?
Well, you tell me in accented English,
'The little guy in the middle is the loser.'
The devil spins around and flashes us a smile
like Al Pacino. I chant Ó'Flatharta's ode to the cregg,
which flowers as we roam the island.
Small fields of primroses and gentians
have the terrible freshness of lost children.

Here sweet accidents are married to hard labour.
Poets make uneasy pagans.
Chiapas, you say, Chiapas, and tell me
that in Mexico there would be red earth.
'And scorpions to give the line bite.'
We have sirens and seashells in common
though later at Dun Aengus I angle
my body out from the clefts in the limestone

in case. This small stone citadel
is no match for Oaxaca or Macchu Picchu
but it serves the same purpose –

as good a place as any to start the past,
to offer gifts of older Gods,
Celtic or Mayan, it doesn't matter;
they are idols of our own desire to comfort
those who swept up the mess
left by torture, emigration, famine,
again and again and again. The ones that were left.
There must have been more to their lives than this,
we think, they must have had simple faith,
if only in the dead partying along the seashore,
the caoin of a guitar, white roses on the water.

Craft

It's all about knowing when
to cut the nets on a fine
catch and run before disaster
and when to risk the vessel
for a haul of silver.

Canvas Currach II

The black canvas drawn like a dress
over the ribs is skin this time.
Not even a treacherous shift
separates her from the waves.

The people on this coast know the sea
holds or gives up whom she will
and yields occasional miracles – coral,
gold coins, ambergris.

She shoulders up the lumps of water
between her and sanctuary
as good as the oarsmen she has drawn;
they are her luck, and the red-tipped oars

dip like fingers into a sea of bones.
She makes shore. Now all depends
on what they call this sleek stranger –
jetsam or treasure.